Succeeding in E-Commerce

"Insider" Advice and Practical Tips

by Rodrigo Alhadeff

Table of Contents

4

Chapter

1

Preface

The idea for this book came up during one of the training courses I usually conduct to explain advanced uses of Comersus shopping cart.

While referring to specific features of the software, it dawned on me that many of the topics I was dealing with were not limited to the Comersus shopping cart at all; rather, they could be applied to virtually any website with an online sales channel.

Then I thought: "layout integration, security, support, payment gateways, shipping quotes, fraud, eGoods... it's a shame that all this valuable information can only be accessed by users who attend the courses".

It's true that there are many books on e-commerce out there, but most have been written by people who never had any hands-on experience dealing with the real issues that come up when trying to implement an online store. Concepts that are presented from a purely theoretical standpoint and are not grounded in experience prove to be merely general advice that is impracticable or outdated. Even worse, it may be both impracticable *and* outdated!

This book is intended as a useful tool for anyone

planning or managing an e-commerce site. You may arrive at the same conclusions on your own through trial and error, but why damage your reputation and waste time and money in the process? Many companies have been successfully selling online for years; you can capitalize on their experience. This book is the result of many years of applying e-commerce and witnessing the achievements and failures of companies big and small in their attempts to implement online selling.

The chapters in this book are self-contained. If digital goods don't apply to your industry, simply skip that chapter and move on. Or, if you are particularly interested in one topic, you may jump to that section and start there. However, if you have no hurry or preferences, I suggest you follow the order of the book for a clear and progressive flow of ideas.

Whatever your approach to the book, I am confident you will find the contents straightforward, useful, and enjoyable.

Rodrigo Alhadeff

Chapter 2

Site Design, Contents and Structure

Planning

The design of your website is not a minor issue. Neither is it unrelated to the e-commerce functionality you wish to implement. You might think that with reasonable prices and considerable traffic you will still sell, regardless of web design. While you may be right, take this thought with you: sloppy web design will surely translate into lower sales.

So, what is the best way to go? Hiring a professional design company for the job? Placing a generic template? Should the shopping cart be adapted for your design, or the other way round? Is Flash better than static HTML?

To plan for your ideal e-commerce site, try to think of what *you* like finding when you shop online.

What elements do you like? For example:

- Fast-loading pages
- Easy access to basic links from any screen

Which elements hinder a pleasant shopping

experience? For example:

- Lack of user-friendliness
- No search box

Get a list together to set your priorities.

With the list ready, you can put together a basic blueprint for your site. How? Get a blank sheet of paper, draw a frame to represent the first screen of your store (home page), and start dividing the screen in sections for different content.

You will probably want your products to occupy center stage. Assign to them the appropriate space, and then add a search box, a category list, a special offers section, and anything you think a good home page should include.

In publishing, but also in the movements of shoppers in brick-and-mortar stores and their attention in websites, there is a concept called *rightward drift*. That is why advertising on the right pages of publications is more expensive, and that is why brick-and-mortar stores place their key goods to the right of entrances. Take a cue from them, and remember the potential of the right side of your site for displaying key products or any other information that is significant for your business.

Did you know that...? On the home pages of leading e-commerce sites, product images take up at least 25% of the area viewed by average users without scrolling.

Then take another sheet of paper to design the product details page, including variations (customer selections such as color and size), cross selling (offering related products to the customer), the way you would like to display images, the space assigned to product description, and a space where quantity is specified, if applicable.

Another important screen is the shopping cart page, where the customer will view the information for all the products they have added to the cart. This information includes total amounts and sometimes also estimated shipping costs and recommended related products.

Modify your original schema by implementing these suggestions. Your company's logo is vital for your online identity, find the best place for it at the header or a side bar. If you have a legacy logo that is unsuitable for a web site, hire a designer to enhance its color, weight and appeal for the Internet.

A navigation menu that is present on all pages is also important, and it should include links to basic information that any shopper is likely to need: Contact

Us, About Us, Security and Privacy Policy, and links to basic features such as Home, Categories, Search, View Cart and Checkout.

> Note about the menu: it should be clear and visible, but it must be "lighter" than other parts of the design so that it doesn't steal the spotlight from what is most important: your products.

Now that you have your blueprint on paper you can either look for a template that fits your vision, or hire a professional designer to develop a custom look. Make sure you have your ideas in order prior to contacting a designer. Some designers have their own agendas; if, for example, your designer has been lately fascinated with the possibilities of Flash animation as illustrated in a magazine on minimalist trends, you just might end up with a home page featuring no more than a giant grapefruit, with no text in sight. As extreme as this example may seem, be prepared for this type of situation and for imposing your vision over your designer's preferences.

Also note that your schema could give way to a broad range of possible designs. It is a good idea to follow the progress in the design to make sure that it is going in the right direction.

Another element to look out for during the progress of the design is simplicity. Keep in mind that the purpose of your site's visitors will be to purchase products or services, and all graphic components must aid this main objective. Eye-catching animation technologies such as Flash and DHTML are available, but thinking back to your own experience at the most popular online stores, and even portals and search engines: Do they make use of such technologies? Do they abuse them? Or, on the contrary, are you noticing a back-to-basics trend?

A simple design will also keep loading time low, allowing pages to load quickly and providing a more pleasant shopping experience. Browse the net for tips on the maximum weight recommended for web pages and the maximum time a page should take to load. You might rest on the fact that most shoppers use broadband and high-end resources, but there are still many other factors affecting browsing speed, such as your own site's loading time, intermediate steps in the connection between your site and the user's machine, and other simultaneous tasks such as downloading mp3 files and watching a movie online. Therefore, use simplicity to your advantage to optimize the speed and performance of your site. Remember shoppers hate waiting, and the end to their frustration at long waiting times is just a click away.

Note: There is another issue affecting loading times. Even if your site has optimized graphics and HTML, it may still take long to load. Why? Too much interaction, and not enough planning. If you add a dynamic list of best-selling products that is updated every time your home page is visited, the database will collapse, slowing down the whole site. Limit this type of query to internal pages, where visitors are bound to be fewer. Also consider implementing a utility to update the best sellers list once a day and ease the burden on the database.

You will likely require professional esthetic assistance beyond the web design proper. Merchants will typically purchase a digital camera to take pictures of their products and display them on the store, but then a sleek design will be ruined by amateurish pictures that turn shoppers off, at least in the cases of products that are "sold" visually. If you resell products, which is often the case if you sell electronics or computer goods, you may be able to get high-quality product images from your supplier or the manufacturer. Prefer these to your homemade pictures.

If professional pictures are not readily available, seriously consider hiring a photographer who will use the right lighting and equipment to present your products as they deserve.

Merchants selling software and other digital goods cannot afford to overlook design either. The right design of a software box can significantly enhance sales since shoppers have the need to visually represent their purchase, even if the product is delivered by download, where there actually is no box to be shipped or received.

The same applies to services, where it is advisable to design a related image such as a padlock for security services or a folder for a business incorporation service.

Design, Contents and Navigation

After discussing some basic planning and organization, let's turn now to recommendations for design, contents and navigation, which are useful both for new sites and existing sites to be modified. If you are building your site from scratch, the design process will be seamless. Otherwise, you might have to modify some aspects of your existing site, but your trouble will be worth it. In e-commerce, wise decisions can be clearly measured in terms of income.

Design

DIY: Not A Good Idea

If you need to design a website, hire an experienced web designer or purchase a professional template. Your e-commerce site is not the right place to experiment with DIY tools. There are plenty of software applications available for web design that are attractive due to their ease of use, but the outcome will be anything but attractive if you don't have the skills to use them wisely.

Here is an example I'm particularly fond of: a few years ago I traveled to Brazil to perform a Comersus installation for a large company with an online sales channel. I had been told there was already a web design in place by one of their specialists: "The Engineer". I thought it was some sort of inner joke, a nickname for the web designer due to his attention to detail. But, when I received the CD with the design, I realized this "work of art" had really been designed by an engineer, more specifically an electronics specialist, as I learnt later on. I then contacted the company to make sure this was the design they had in mind - some header images weighed over 8mb, colors were not clearly defined, just to mention a few features - and they explained: "We considered that an engineer has longer studies than a web designer, and of course they can use FrontPage, so we gave this job to one of the company engineers to lower costs".

Less Is More

Your design should be nice, but mostly practical. When a page is too crowded, the visitor's eyes will take longer to find what they need or to get the most important message you are trying to get across.

To see for yourself, go to one of the websites called "portals", and answer the following questions quickly: Where is the navigation bar? What is the submenu used for? Where do I start? What is the main section?

Then, go straight to the point. Don't crowd your pages with unnecessary text, links or images. Don't insist on plenty of images just because they look nice. Every image or graphic you include must serve a purpose.

Ad-like Graphics

Avoid graphics or images that look like ads, even if they are!

Remember that surfers have learnt to automatically ignore anything remotely resembling an ad, as a consequence of constant abuse of banners and buttons. Make sure you don't scare a potential buyer away, just when you are trying to get their attention.

Don't use internal graphics that look by banners, whether by format or location. Don't use aggressive animations with blinking images or too many colors that are not related to your site, or any kind of animation that looks like an ad.

Home Page Updating

Don't expect users returning to your e-commerce site to be ready to rake through endless pages for new content. They won't, even if you add the obsolete caption "Last Updated on...". You must refer to new content yourself on the home page, by placing direct links to new contents, with or without graphics.

Design and maintain your home page as if you would a store window. Highlight the sections you wish your visitors to see, and use design to lead them. Use visit tracking software to determine your visitors' average return time. Then update your content in such a way that they will know your store will have something new for them every so often, for example each month, whether it is a new product, offer, information, or even design.

Web Graphics

It seems obvious to point it out at this stage, but there are still websites that look like they were designed for printed brochures. Optimize your e-commerce site's graphics and photos for the web! Pay attention to weight and format.

Tip: If you add photos, use "jpg" format. It supports better weight and image quality control. Make sure you set them to progressive image so that users can see the image as it loads. Use "gif" format for graphics or drawings with plain colors (not gradients).

Another basic recommendation: cut images. This helps general viewing and loading of the page.

Contents

Think Online

When writing up content for your e-commerce site think "online", not "for print".
Use simple language and avoid pompous or fancy expressions. Keep your paragraphs short (bullets are a great resource here) and highlight important words or concepts to help visitors visually focus on the main ideas you are trying to get across.

The Inverted Pyramid For Long Texts

When writing texts that are longer than usual but must be included in your site without exceptions, in sections such as "About Us" or "Terms and Conditions", or even in some product descriptions, use the inverted pyramid writing technique.

Present the information in the following order:
1) Conclusion
2) Main information
3) General and context information

Spelling

Check your spelling for mistakes! What is your reaction when you come across spelling or punctuation mistakes in a book or newspaper? Online texts are no different in this respect. Don't treat the quality of your spelling any different just because it is not on paper. Proofread your texts before going live; hire the services of a proofreader or writer if necessary.

Note: For extensive information on writing product descriptions refer to the Pro-Sales Item Display section.

Comprehensive Texts

It is valid to publish your products' basic facts and let customers find out themselves about shipping fees and payment methods during checkout. After all, they can always send an e-mail if they want this information in advance. The same applies to refund and support policies. However, consider that customers hate to ask unnecessary questions, and they will probably doubt your ability to answer in a timely fashion. Make all necessary information readily available so that your customers don't feel frustrated at not finding it online. Don't reply completely on the possibility of e-mail and contact form inquiries.

Navigation

The 3 Clicks Rule

If it takes visitor more than 3 clicks to access any popular section of your site, you probably need to rethink the organization of your site.

Keep it simple. Just one click to access main sections is the ideal scenario. If you have no choice but to divide information further, make sure more than 3 clicks are not necessary to get to what's important.

Visited Pages

If you use hypertext, always change the color of links already visited. This small detail does a lot for site navigability: it saves the user time, mostly in sites were links are in abundance. The user will have an idea of which links remain to be seen and will be able to avoid visiting the same link twice.

Coherence

Make sure the main navigation bar occupies a fixed space throughout all sections of your site. Keep the navigation bar fixed on all pages.

Don't place unnecessary buttons:

- Many sites display a "Home" button on the Home Page. It may be convenient for design management, but consider this is a nuisance for visitors, who are presented with a completely superfluous link.
- Does your site really need a "search" function? If you have 4 products, or 10 pages with content, probably not. If you have a large catalog of products or over 100 pages with content, the answer is yes. Weigh in these variables before placing a content or product search function on your site.

Flash Navigation

Do you need a Flash navigation menu? Fair enough, but make sure it doesn't take ages to load! The menu is a basic element that must be available as soon as you enter a site.

Design, The Big No-Nos

Pop-Up Windows

Don't use them at all. Even when the latest versions of browsers warn users of pop-up windows and request consent before displaying the, users feel invaded and close the windows without ever checking its content.

> Tip: If you want to highlight something, do it on the same page.

Horizontal Scrolling

Horizontal scrolling works against your design. The user will not see the whole picture at once, they will have to scroll to discover any more information, and navigation will be hampered.

> Tip: 760 pixels is the maximum recommended page width for the best visibility in 800x 600 or better configurations.

PDF Documents

PDF documents are usually created from printable materials such as user guides or any other document with a large number of pages. Adding PDF files to your site will be a mistake, since they cut the flow of navigation. They are usually heavy and confusing for online browsing.

> Tip: Wherever possible, convert your PDF files to HTML pages. If the length of a document makes this impossible, make it clear for the user in the link that they are about to open a PDF file, or enable the file for download instead of opening within the browser.

Flash, 360° Images, and Other Applications

These technologies are not forbidden offhand, since their use will only be relevant or not depending on the nature of your site. Remember the following: don't use them just to follow a trend or brag about your mastery of new technologies. Make a conscious decision on the convenience of using them.

Flash

Ask yourself the following questions before implementing Flash animation on your site:

1) Does your product or service need to be presented in a spectacular way?
2) Is your business related to audiovisual arts (design, cinema, video, audio, etc)?
3) Is it absolutely necessary to showcase your product or service with animation, or will a graph or photo do the trick?

> Tip: Users are not known for their
> patience, even if you place a "preloader"
> before each Flash animation. Make sure it's
> worth their trouble.

360° Images

This is an interesting and useful tool if your e-commerce site deals with sceneries or spaces, for example in hotels, real estate, and architecture. Also consider it if you need to display products or machinery from several angles.

If this does not apply to your site, then there is no point in implementing 360° images.

Chapter

3

The Shopping Cart

The shopping cart is the main element of any e-commerce site. In a nutshell, a shopping is an application that allows customers to select products from your catalog, calculate tax and other additional fees such as shipping charges, and finally pay for them.

The shopping carts available today support a wider array of features, including newsletter distribution, auctions, and sales forecasting. That is why you should consider our choice carefully.

The first choice to make is: Should I go for a shopping cart as a service, or purchase a shopping cart application?

Shopping cart services have the following advantages:

1) Very low cost, in some cases even free
2) No complicated installation
3) Several hosting companies and payment gateways offer shopping cart services as an interesting way to get started, since they significantly reduce the hassles of setting up a store dealing with several separate providers.

Shopping cart services have the following disadvantages:

1) If you change your hosting or payments provider – or if you switch from whichever company has offered you the shopping cart – you will probably not be able to keep your cart. Even worse, you may not be able to export your products and customer information to a new system.

2) Customization capabilities are usually limited. You can change the header and footer, but what if you want to simplify the checkout process or add a field to a database table? You will probably have to conform to a fairly rigid schema.

3) The service providers will have access to your customers' information and to any confidential information in your database. If they wanted to get this information, they could.

4) In the event of a security threat you will depend on the provider's technicians to update the application, and you will not be able to solve the problem yourself.

5) Paying a monthly fee for a shopping cart service may be impractical compared to a shopping cart application, where there are usually no monthly fees but only a one-time purchase price.

6) There is usually limited space for publishing products and for storing customer history.

All these issues seem to be solved if you choose a shopping cart application, but don't think this is ideal either. You should weigh the pros and cons of each approach.

Shopping cart applications are programs that usually reside in the same server where your web site is installed.

Here are some of their advantages:

1) Full customizability, and usually the possibility of complete manipulation of the application.
2) A wider range of features available.
3) Very low cost compared to monthly fees, in some cases even free.
4) A wide range of payment methods available. E-commerce services usually offer 1 to 10 gateways, while most popular applications are now supporting around 70 payment gateways.

The main disadvantages of shopping cart applications are:

1) Installation requires some basic technical skills.
2) Due to the large number of configuration and customization options, it may take longer to set up an application than a service.

Of course, shopping cart companies offer paid installation services for their applications, and most offer hosting services as well, where the shopping cart is preinstalled.

My recommendation, then, is the following: if you are just getting started, you will offer few products, under 10 orders are expected per day, and you don't have the skills to transfer files by FTP, you should consider signing up for a shopping cart service. Otherwise, you will surely draw more benefits from a shopping cart application.

If you decide to go for a shopping cart application, take into account the following variables:

1) Does the cart run on Windows and/or Linux servers?
2) What database does it require?
3) Is your hosting plan compatible with the cart's requirements?
4) Does the cart include source code? Or is it an executable application?

Your web site will probably reside on a Windows or Unix/Linux server, so make sure any application you look into is compatible with your environment. If your server is Unix/Linux you may need a mySQL database. In the case of Windows, your database choices will probably include Access and SQL Server, and maybe mySQL as well.

The database is where all of your application's data will be stored, including customer information, catalog information, and sales history, among others.

Note: A few shopping carts work without a database, but their use is quite limited to very small stores, so I will not discuss them here.

The database you use will also condition your project's scaling. A shopping cart that only supports Access will only be suitable for stores with limited products and visits. If you expect your business to grow, prefer an application that will also support professional databases such as SQL Server and mySQL.

Basic shopping cart requirements can be grouped into three categories:

1) Scripting programming language
2) Database
3) Additional components

The most popular scripting languages are ASP for Windows servers, and PHP for Linux. If your server supports the scripting language indicated by the shopping cart, you shouldn't have trouble executing it.

Note: You can also execute ASP on Linux and PHP on Windows, but this option is not standard in most hosting plans.

Also check the database supported, since basic hosting plans sometimes don't include professional databases or require an additional fee.

Lastly, shopping carts can require certain components for specific functions such as sending e-mail, web uploading, export to Excel, real-time shipping quotes, and some component-based gateways such as LinkPoint API, for example.

Some shopping carts are executable: they don't provide source code but .exe or .dll files to be installed on the server. If you use shared hosting, you probably won't be able to use them. Also consider that these shopping carts pose most of the same problems as shopping cart services, especially related to lack of flexibility.

Choosing the right shopping cart seems like a daunting task: a service or an application, multiple servers, multiple databases, multiple programming languages, executables or scripting languages…and we haven't got to the actual features yet.

When e-commerce was still in its infancy, shopping carts were limited to the very basic functions of presenting a catalog, compiling products, calculating tax, and taking payments. Today, such functions are still at the core of what a shopping cart is, but numerous advanced features have been added. Some of the most sophisticated features are wap access to catalogs, fraud prevention subsystems, newsletters, and recommendations based on purchase history, to name a few.

Such a variety of features only makes it harder to choose a shopping cart. However, you can use a simple method to categorize features into necessary, desirable, and irrelevant, based on your industry and your e-commerce needs. Of course limits can be blurry, but it is fairly safe to say that digital goods distribution will be irrelevant to a clothing store, just like shipping quotes will be irrelevant to a software download store. We will then offer specific advice for any store, tangible goods stores, digital goods stores, retail and wholesale stores, resellers of popular products, and internationally-oriented stores.

This will provide a practical framework for guidance, since most stores will fall into one of the groups.

Any And All Stores

Control Panel

The Control Panel is of vital importance to any store. This is where products are loaded and modified, order details can be viewed, special offers are configured, and many other tasks are carried out. Therefore, a good control panel must be intuitive, user friendly, and dynamic.

Imagine a rigid control panel where you need to go through a staggering 10 screens to add a product. Management tasks will be difficult and money- and time-consuming. The same applies to control panels that require additional tools, such as FTP clients, to upload product images. For each product you will need to FTP the image, remember the file name, and assign it to the product. It may not seem too terrible for a small store, but it will be nightmarish if your catalog is large.

Then it is a good idea to take some time to visit the

online demo for the shopping cart you are interested in. Make sure that you like the organization, and check that repetitive tasks follow some logic and optimized steps. If several people on your staff will be using the control panel, check that you can create user profiles with different permissions – you don't want a dispatcher to access your whole customers database.

The control panel is also the point of entry to your store. Anyone who can gain access will have full control of every aspect and all information. If an intruder accesses your control panel, they will post offensive messages on your website, in the best-case scenario. In the worst-case scenario, they will steal your customer database and blackmail you not to use that information…So the control panel is not a minor factor when choosing a shopping cart. Proper security measures must be available to prevent unauthorized access. It is usual for current control panels to store a log with the most recent admin access and block access to profiles with many login failures, in order to prevent brute force attacks. Some even allow installation on local networks with no external access, or customization for compliance with the company's security standards.

Did you know that…? Brute force is a system used to gain access to password-protected areas. The method is quite simple: all possible password combinations are entered, until access is ultimately gained.

An Attractive Catalog

A clever organization and convenient access to the products in your catalogue can make the difference between selling and not selling. While potential customers may reach the store through a specific product link, very often this first approach then creates interest for other categories and products. Therefore, it is important for your shopping cart to allow listings by category, suppliers, best sellers, and new arrivals, among others, as well as allow you to present your products in attractive ways, for example with several images, HTML formatting for product details, user reviews, external links, etc.

Compatibility with Search Engines and Other Advertising Systems

A solid, functional store is no good without any customers willing to purchase products from it. Today, most online traffic is driven by search engines that rank contents based on the inner organization of web pages (keywords, metatags, title, etc), so a good shopping cart must include the tools necessary to achieve good rankings that translate to traffic to the store. Another related feature is integration with price comparison engines such as Pricegrabber, Shopping.com, and Froogle.

Note: For extensive information on increasing traffic refer to the Increasing Sales section.

Variations

Variations are options available for a base product. The typical example would be color and size for a piece of clothing, but variations apply to all kinds of products, even digital. For example, software can be offered boxed or for download.

Shopping carts must support variations groups for products; otherwise you would have to load one item for each combination of variations, and you would end up with multiple items that are in fact the same product.

Import And Export

The developers of certain e-commerce applications don't offer import or export tools, usually as part of a strategy to keep their users captive. As a customer, you should demand these tools that will offer you the chance to choose freely in the future. If you ever want to switch products, whether to an in-house development or a better third-party application, the availability of migration tools will make the process much smoother.

Import and export tools are also useful for integrating the shopping cart to other systems, such as external listings and billing facilities.

Tangible Goods Stores

Stock Management

All shopping carts should offer reliable stock management. Imagine the consequences for your company's reputation if you sold products that are not actually in your possession. Consider that the fact that a product is added to the cart doesn't necessarily mean it should be deducted from stock, since the purchase might not be finalized. Check that you can manage stock in combination with all your systems, thanks to import and export functions, and that stock is updated at the right step. Detailed stock management also enables offers such as "last chance, x items left in stock".

Efficient stock management should include not only stock levels but also other variables such as: minimum acceptable stock levels for each product, restock costs, quantity discounts, availability time, etc. Then the shopping cart will perform complex calculations that result in the best times for restocking, and ultimately assure that your customers will always have your products in stock and ready for purchase.

The most complete shopping carts also support automatic restock requests when stock drops to a certain level. For example, if your store experiences unusually high sales of a product on a Saturday, the shopping cart alone can request restocking, and at noon on Monday the new products will be waiting on your doorstep.

Accurate Shipping Quotes

If your store carries tangible goods, it must offer an accurate real-time shipping quotes system. Customers happy about good prices will actually abandon their purchase if they encounter high shipping fees. And, high shipping fees may be the result of deficient quoting, whether the shopping cart lacks real-time quoting or doesn't use all the product's data (including weight and size) to calculate shipping costs. Also note many stores offer discounted shipping, or free shipping for certain products. Customers expect to find this kind of benefit, and the shopping cart must be able to provide it.

Digital Goods Stores

Secure Distribution

Distribution is the key to any digital store. Stores selling digital goods must protect their greatest assets, so they can't afford to deliver static links for software download, since they will be out of business as soon as their products become publicly available. MP3 songs, licensed software, photos, and other digital goods require secure download systems where links are available for a limited number of days and accessed only be customers within the store. Links should not point to the real location of the file, but to a fictitious and temporary location. This can be achieved with download obfuscators or dynamic creation of ZIP files that are then deleted.

When it comes to distributing software serials or calling card codes, for example, the shopping cart should maintain a product-specific code database and distribute codes as sales come in.

You might think that, since you have very few sales, you can create and distribute serials manually, but I suggest you choose a shopping cart with the tools described. If your business grows in the future, you won't have to switch applications due to an unwise first choice. Also consider customers tend to lose patience if software is not received immediately, or they simply choose not to shop where immediate download is not offered.

Manual Order Approval

It is a known fact that criminals prefer to post fraudulent orders on digital goods stores, since they receive the product immediately and they are less likely to be caught and prosecuted.

Some stores with moderate sales will not risk distributing products before a manual review of orders, and sometimes even confirming the legitimacy of the order by phone or other methods.

The best shopping cart for this scenario should support checking orders from the control panel and approving the distribution of goods manually.

Disabled Shipping

As obvious as it may seem, there is no shipping in digital goods stores, so you should be able to remove any related step from the checkout process. Customers who are forced to go through unnecessary steps might abandon the purchase.

Purchase drive is a short period of time during which a potential buyer is willing to purchase a certain product online. This drive is followed by some moment of inertia when, even while doubting the need or convenience of the product, they are still willing to go through with the purchase. It is very important for the shopping cart to let this impulse flow with as few obstacles as possible until the transaction is completed.

Simplified Checkout

If you read about *purchase drive* above, you are probably reflecting on how many unnecessary steps could be removed from the checkout process. The shopping cart should allow modification of the checkout procedure to adapt it to specific needs and, even better, to reduce it as much as possible. Some shopping carts offer One Step Checkout, the ideal schema, out of the box. In the case of software, it is even preferable to add the fields for credit card information right on the product page, so that it can be purchased immediately with no need to go through complicated registration, checkout, shipping and discount code screens.

Retail And Wholesale Stores

Price Management

In this type of store, it is important to assign the right price to each customer type. Some shopping carts are not suitable for retail and wholesale scenarios and try to patch this lack of functionality by applying a global discount code to wholesale customers. This workaround only makes he cart more difficult to use. A suitable system should present the right price to each customer, and in some cases also hide wholesale prices from retail customers.

It must also be possible to assign arbitrary prices to wholesale customers. Shopping cart developers rarely consider this option, but it is very useful in practice, especial for promotions or building customer loyalty.

Different Payment and Shipping Methods

Stores that cater both to retail and wholesale customers usually face the challenge of maintaining two wholly different, but parallel, scenarios with different pricing, payment methods, shipping methods, tax rules, and even products. The shopping cart must be prepared to display these variables based on customer type. Business with wholesalers is usually more personal; there has probably been communication prior to the online transaction, and e-commerce is used for purchases simply for convenience. More flexible payment terms are usually available to wholesalers, for example Cash on Delivery or Bill me Later.

A practical way to achieve the functionality described is with separate storefronts connected to the same database. Some advanced shopping carts support this schema, including filtering reports and all other data per store and maintaining different layouts. The wholesale store is sometimes password-protected as well.

Resellers of Popular Products

Export to Price Comparison Engines

Stores that sell products available for purchase at multiple other online stores have a difficult time competing and getting traffic. Why would anyone want to buy from MyBrandNewStore.com, when Amazon.com carries the exact same thing? There is one main reason: price. You can compete by offering lower prices. But, how can you publicize them? Through price comparison engines. They allow merchants to load their products and selling prices at regular intervals. So, when a customer is interested in a digital camera, for example, they will use these engines to try and get the same product at a better price elsewhere.

Where do shopping carts come in? While it is possible to load products manually for comparison, it is far from practical, especially considering the listing must be updated with each change in stock or pricing. Therefore, the shopping cart should support exporting your product database to price comparison engines. This seemingly insignificant feature can be a deal maker or breaker for stores reselling popular products.

Internationally-Oriented Stores

Regionalization

Online stores oriented to the international market clearly must support quoting for international shipments, and international payment methods.

But this is not enough. Foreign customers will want to know the price of products in their local currencies, and they may have to be presented with product descriptions and store policies in their own languages.

Therefore, check for the following features in a shopping cart: multicurrency or currency conversion, store language selection, and multilanguage product descriptions and screen messages. But that is not all. Many stores support a Multilanguage schema but don't provide the actual translations, you may have to hire professional translation services for each language you want available on your store. And, even if the store is readily translated to the languages you need, you will still have to translate the merchant-specific content such as product details and store policies.

Just like in the case of retail and wholesale stores, the ideal situation is to connect multiple storefronts to one database. This will enable you not only to translate the store, but also to display stores that are different in many other aspects including language, layout, and product selection (certain products are not exported, whether by law or convenience).

Pro-Sales Item Display

Your ultimate purpose is to sell, and any action you perform on your store can bring you closer to or farther from your target. The way you display your products is key. I have already mentioned that the esthetic of your site and store in general should be uniform, attractive, and lead visitors' attention to the sections you deem most important. The same applies to each individual product. Even if your design looks professional and you have covered all variables discussed in the Site Design section, a deficient product display probably means your sales are lower than they could be.

The concept of pro-sales display approaches efficient display as much more than a list of features, and it recognizes both an objective element comprising descriptions and also a subjective element.

Let's take a look at both.

The Objective Element in Pro-Sales Display

It includes the name of the product and its code, packaging, technical specs and requirements, and its main image representing the product as a whole.

Many store owners believe the objective element in

pro-sales display covers all the needs of product description in a store.

In fact, purchase decisions are in part based on emotions, not only on objective data. So, if your store only presents the objective element of product display, based on rational criteria, you will be neglecting a factor that can make or break a purchase decision.

The Subjective Element in Pro-Sales Display

In contrast with the objective element, the subjective element doesn't deal with listing product features but with adding value that can make a difference for a potential buyer.

A basic approach includes projecting pleasant scenarios derived from purchasing the product or service offered.

For example, instead of merely listing the technical specs of a Rolex Air-King watch, you will stress the qualities of the owner of such watch.

"The owner of a Rolex Air-King is a person who makes important decisions and appreciates reliability and flexibility. Whether it is a business meeting in Tokyo, or a tennis match with friends, the owner of a Rolex Air-King knows he will always be there on time".

Note: Each store owner should assess the type of discourse related to the products or services offered. If you offer screwdrivers, it us unlikely that you will be able to base your subjective element on the status gained by owners of your products. Or, maybe you will, but this will not be relevant to purchase decisions. This case probably calls for exploring qualities of productivity or versatility, rather than status.

Of course pro-sales display means much more than this and covers many methods. One of them is creatively turning disadvantages into positive qualities. For example, if you sell a cheap Z1 computer sound card, you can describe it as follows:

"The Z1 sound card is ideal for the office, where it is important for the computer to issue notification sounds. Needless to say, this 8 bit card delivers efficient and clear reproduction of wav files common in business applications, and will make your staff think twice about using computer audio for entertainment".

Another method is stressing advantages:

"The Z1 sound card is compatible with a broad range of operating systems and drivers are installed automatically, with no need for CDs or update downloads. Why waste your time on last generation cards that require lots of time for configuration? Install the Z1 and forget about complicated procedures

that only a specialist could
understand".

The above description focuses on ease of installation
and never mentions the possible poor performance of
the sound card, that can be deduced from the listing of
objective specifications.

Lastly, it is very useful to anticipate yourself to
potential objections. If you sell a laser printer that is
more expensive than your competitor's, you know
that price will be the first objection of a potential
buyer. Why pay more than I have to? A clever
presentation will be the following:

"We have made a decision to launch a
printer that is slightly more
expensive than the competition's but
includes a toner cartridge with
significantly higher printing
capacity. The cost of toner should
not be neglected. After three years
of use, you will have spent 40% more
on toner if you choose the
competitor's printer. It is your
choice: pay a bit more now, or a lot
more tomorrow".

You can see here clearly that the subjective element is
not simply a personal opinion, but a conclusion
derived from features already informed as part of the
objective element in the display of a product.
Potential customers can in fact deduce future savings
by comparing technical specs, but they usually don't
have the knowledge to perform such comparison, or
they simply ignore that toners for printers are pricey.

In some stores, you will see that the subjective description of a product may work against another product sold there as web. Consider that this is not ideology but business, and it is perfectly valid. In fact, the decision is ultimately in the hands of the customer, who feels more or less attracted by the subjective description of each product.

For example, you may well offer a slimming product packaged in small bags and focus on how practical it is to carry it in your pocket and forget about extenuating exercise, and at the same time offer an exercise bike and focus on the benefits of losing weight naturally without chemicals. Customers will feel attracted to one of these products based on their profile and lifestyle, and there is no need to establish a unique ideology that applies to your whole catalog.

Practical Example

```
Shaver
Brand: Johnson
Model: TR12
Rechargeable: no
Power: batteries
Trimmer: no
Color: yellow
Price: $22
```

This simple list of features will make it difficult for many potential buyers to feel purchase drive toward the TR12 shaver, but applying the recommendations above we can present the product in the following way:

"Johnson TR12 shaver has cutting-edge design with curved lines and vibrant yellow colors. It is ideal for young men who cherish their sleeping time and want to be able to shave in the elevator, in the car or on the bus. The days of having to find a power outlet or recharging regularly are over. The TR12 works with regular batteries. Operation is as simple as pushing a button. The size of its blade makes it practical for shaving, shaping sideburns, and touching up crew cuts."

Chapter

5

Payment Methods

During the first stages of e-commerce the options to receive payments were very limited. Today, there are literally thousands of services available that are widely known as payment gateways. So, how can you choose the gateway that's right for you?

First, you should draw a line between payment gateways which require a merchant account and those which don't.

Payment gateways requiring a merchant account usually have the following advantages:

- Attractive commission rates, for example 1.8% of each transaction, a fixed $0.20 from each transaction, and a series of monthly charges grouped under several headings, usually amounting to less than $100. This means that your company keeps a greater share of gross sales.
- A more professional image to present to your customers, since credit card charges appear under the name of your company.
- More flexibility for integration with a shopping cart, enabling customers to place payments seamlessly, without ever leaving the store.

On the other hand, payment gateways requiring a merchant account have several disadvantages:

- They seldom engage in fraud prevention and rather leave it in the hands of the seller to decide which transactions are safe to accept and which should be rejected. If the company suffers a high rate of fraud, the gateway provider may terminate the service.
- Signing up for a merchant account can take around one month.
- Merchant accounts are usually only granted to incorporated companies with an existing financial background.
- It can be hard to get authorization for transactions with certain credit cards such as American Express and Diners Club.

In the case of payment gateways not requiring a merchant account, the main advantages are:

- You will be ready to sell immediately.
- Fraud prevention tools are provided free of charge. Since payment system providers are the actual merchants, it is in their best interest to minimize fraud and avoid problems with credit cards. Whatever the reason, you win: a lower risk of fraud, at no additional cost.
- There are usually no fixed charges (only a commission over transactions).

Of course the disadvantages are:

- A less attractive commission rate, usually between 5.5% and 12%, with a $0.80 fixed rate per transaction.

- The name on the customer's credit card statement will be the name of the payment company, not yours.
- The customer's credit card data is not stored with you, but with the payment gateway.

Another factor to bear in mind is that some payment gateways are not available for the sale of intangibles such as software and services, while others are.

From the point of view of technology, you should consider the type of integration and security measures offered by each gateway.

The ideal situation for quick implementation is Web Form integration with the payment gateway: integration simply consists of a web form to send payment information.

If you would rather have a more secure and uniform integration, you can choose a gateway with a more complex integration method. However, first check with your webmaster that you comply with all requirements, usually including the following:

- Purchasing and installing an SSL certificate.
- Permission to install proprietary gateway components.
- Permission to open certain ports in the firewall.

SSL stands for Secure Socket Layer. In a nutshell, an SSL certificate identifies the merchant or the owner of the website and encrypts the data passed between the customer's browser and the server. SSL is mostly used on the pages where the customer enters credit card information. In order to avoid theft of credit card numbers, the information is encrypted and sent to the server, where it is decrypted and used to charge a purchase.

Verisign and Thawte are two popular SSL providers. 128-bit certificates cost around $99 a year.

If your website is hosted on a shared server, you will typically need to add a fee for certificate installation. Once the SSL certificate is in place, you will also be able to use it for other sections of the website where sensitive information is managed, for example customer login and your shopping cart control panel login.

Did you know that...? Many shared hosting companies offer free SSL. As tempting as this may sound, consider that the certificate typically belongs to the hosting company (not yours) and it is installed in a folder outside your hosting account space. Therefore you won't be able to hold a session between the regular location and the SSL location. This means that free SSL is of very little use in practical terms.

Back to payment gateways, we should mention the Call Back Response, Silent Response or Update Script feature. What is this, and how can it help selling with your shopping cart?

Call Back Response is a silent and secure signal sent by the payment gateway to the shopping cart. It notifies the result of the transaction and the order number. Other information that may be notified by the signal includes a transaction ID, date and time of authorization, and fraud indicators, among others.

This is extremely useful to update the order status in your shopping cart from Pending to Paid and trigger other processes related to the approval of a payment, such as:

- Decreasing the stock of the products sold
- Delivering digital goods
- Increasing sales figures
- Notifying affiliates
- Notifying suppliers

In the case that your preferred payment system doesn't support Call Back Response, the shopping cart should allow you to update order status and perform other related processes manually, but this extra task may be tedious and lead to mistakes if there is a high volume of transactions.

Also consider that the fact that your gateway supports Call Back Response does not mean that you have to use it.

Take, for example, a store selling pieces of art. You will surely want to check the transaction manually before alerting the shipping department. In conclusion, Call Back is a desirable feature in a gateway, but you shouldn't feel obligated to use it.

Alternatives to Online Systems

Shopping carts should also support payments through non-traditional means, for example off-line credit cards. This means that the customer's credit card information is stored to be processed later through the usual procedures (POS, phone payment). In some cases, this can be useful if you wish to start selling right away. It can also serve as a backup method if the main online payment system is temporarily unavailable.

Another payment option is PayPal. This company acts as an intermediary between users and transfers funds from one user to another by discounting the amount of the transaction from the payer's account. This system can be useful in certain cases, and it offers many fraud prevention tools to verified PayPal users.

PayPal is also offering a new system called Web Site Payments Pro. It allows you to use PayPal like you would a traditional payment gateway, but it requires installing a personal certificate on the server, and the store is required to channel the checkout through PayPal. That is, customers check out at PayPal and are then redirected to the store. This is PayPal's way of ensuring that more customers will be willing to make payments with existing funds rather than use a credit card.

In terms of security, the tools offered by payment gateways include:

- CVV2 Validation. CVV (short for Card Verification Value) is a code present on credit cards. The codes on Visa, MasterCard and Discover are three digits long and printed on the back of the card. American Express codes are four digits long and printed on the front. This code is supposed to indicate that the purchaser is in possession of the credit card at the time of the transaction. It is not stored along with the rest of the credit card information after a purchase, so it will not go into the wrong hands if a database is stolen.

- AVS Validation. AVS (short for Address Verification System) checks the billing address entered by the customer against the address where the credit card statement is delivered. This system is only available in the US and a few other countries.

- Fraud Ratings. Some gateways use advanced techniques to rate each transaction for risk of fraud, based on the customer's location, the order amount, and other variables. The rating is reported for the merchant to decide whether it is safe to fulfill the order, even if it was originally approved.

- Known Frauder Databases. Some gateways check databases of past frauders to assess the risk of an order, especially in the case of digital goods.

Note: extensive information on fraud prevention in Chapter 9.

Another desirable feature in a payment gateway is support for partial refunds. Why? Suppose your store sells bicycles. Bicycles are notorious for the high cost of shipping them. You have determined in your terms and conditions that, if a product is returned, only the full price of the bicycle will be refunded, not the shipping cost. So, if the bicycle retails at $100, and shipping cost $20, only $100 will be due to the customer. But, if your gateway does not allow you to issue a partial refund on a transaction, you will be forced to refund the full $120. You will lose money and, worse, you will need to adjust your policies due to the gateway's restrictions. You might even conclude that a slightly better discount rate compared to other gateways does not compensate for the money you lose with full refunds. The same applies to subscription services. Suppose a customer subscribes to a 6-month service and requests cancellation at the fifth month. You may be forced to issue a refund for the full 6 months if your gateway does not support partial refunds. Of course you can choose to write a check for the refund, but you should be careful since the customer can request a chargeback on the credit card transaction and cash the check. In general terms, you should always avoid issuing a refund through a means other than the same credit used for the original transaction.

We can conclude that if your store is just starting out you will want to keep fixed costs low. You should choose a gateway that doesn't require your own SSL certificate or installing components in your server, and that doesn't charge excessive penalties for chargebacks.

If your store is already established, with a clear projection of sales levels, you will want to choose a gateway which allows you to use your own merchant account, your own SSL certificate, and offers all the security measures and uniformity of advanced integration methods.

Of course you should also go with a shopping cart that lets you choose. Popular shopping carts usually support over 70 online payment gateways, off-line credit cards, and non-traditional systems such as PayPal and MoneyBookers.

If you experience trouble with the system you have chosen, simply choose again from the extensive list of compatible systems.

Need additional help in choosing a payment system? Refer to the following comparison chart:

Name of the payment system	
Fixed monthly fees	
% discount over each transaction	
Fixed discount over each transaction	
Chargeback penalty	
Number of credit cards accepted	
E-checks accepted within the same system	
Method of layout integration with your site	
SSL provided free of charge	
Call back response	
Security measures	
Types of product allowed	

Chapter 6

Shipping Methods

Just like in the case of payment methods, there are online and offline shipping methods. This means that you can obtain shipping quotes for your store by connecting to the shipper's server and get the exact shipping charge based on weight, size and destination, or calculate charges by means of static rules stored in the shopping cart database.

Real-time shipping quote systems are getting more popular every day, mainly because they are so practical. Why load, configure and store shipping rules, when you can connect to an external system that will produce the exact shipping fee you will pay?

Did you know that...? Customers have sued US e-commerce companies that overcharged for standard shipping services. Differences between actual charges and prices imposed by the companies were verified, resulting in damages paid by the companies to customers. The teaching here is: precision matters.

Consider that most real-time solutions have been designed for companies shipping from the United States, and your shopping cart may not support combining shipping methods; that is, presenting the shopper with a choice between several companies such as DHL, Fedex, UPS, and USPS. Combining options in this way is tricky because the shopping cart has to communicate with each company's server to send package details and parse responses with services and charges available. The time that it takes to gather data from all servers and present a list with all services available combined would be unacceptable waiting time for the shopper.

Simply using real-time shipping quotes doesn't guarantee that the customer will get convenient or suitable shipping charges. Quoting systems require just a few parameters to quote, typically weight, origin, and destination. However, additional information including size, type of destination, type of packaging, and whether pick-up is needed, can result in higher or lower charges. Therefore, it is important to find out the type of integration to the shipping systems offered by the shopping cart, namely which non-required parameters are passed, if any.

Another concern is manipulation of shipping charges. Imagine a case where you wish to add a handling fee or offer a certain product with free shipping. Automatic queries to external systems will not handle such additions and exceptions, and many shopping carts don't support editing the charges received from online quoting systems.

> Did you know that...? Shipping companies typically require shopping carts to communicate with a SOAP request. SOAP is a protocol to send messages by XML through a network. While this requirement is standard, some systems such as Fedex also require proprietary software installed on the store's server, as web as complex certification procedures, before you can start quoting.

If your business model requires offering multiple shipping options from various companies, you should look into services such as Intershipper, that provide multiple quotes in one step. A monthly fee is charged for this service based on the number of transactions, but for large stores the price to pay will be insignificant compared to the benefits of offering customers a wider choice of shipping methods.

With respect to offline quotes, it should first be noted that each store follows a different logic for quoting shipping. They usually don't follow the shippers' rules, whether because they grant a discount on shipping or they charge more to simplify the procedure. In general, the shopping cart should allow configuration based on the most popular parameters – weight and destination- but also other more specific cases such as shipping based on order amount or number of products, and others, even if it is by means of customizing the code.

An interesting option is importing shipping tables from shippers' websites. If your shopping cart supports importing files with current shipping charges, your e-commerce system will find a comfortable middle ground between online and offline systems, since you will enjoy combined, updated services without the complications of manual modifications.

Another concern with both online and offline system is calculating total volume of packages when an order includes more than product. Online systems support sending details for each individual product (weight, length, width, height). By means of complicated algorithms, the shipping company figures the best packaging of goods to minimize cost. In the case of offline quotes, the same kind of calculation must be performed by the shopping cart. Some carts support displaying an estimated charge that is then adjusted manually when an employee actually packages the goods. This is far from ideal: if the actual charge is smaller than the one presented to the customer, the high fee can lead to an abandoned purchase. If the situation is inverted, imagine you are presented with a $10 shipping charge, you complete the online order, and you are later informed that the actual shipping charge is $15. You will probably shop elsewhere in the future.

Sometimes shopping carts are not prepared to perform total volume calculations efficiently. However, they can calculate fairly approximate charges that guarantee the store owner will not lose money when shipping. It is important, in this case, to make it clear to the customer how shipping is calculated, so that they understand possible inaccuracies. If it is common for your store to receive multi-product orders in a market where customers might confirm purchases based on shipping charges, you should consider accurate volume calculation by shipping companies themselves.

The availability of purchased goods can also affect shipping. For the sake of simplicity, you may announce that orders are shipped only when all products in the order become available. Then, if one of the items in an order becomes available three days after purchase, that is when the whole order will be shipped. No doubt this helps simplify shopping cart operation, but if your business requires shipping goods as they become available you should take this into account when choosing a shopping cart. Only a few support combining and dividing shipping within an order by default.

Once goods have been shipped, there is still the matter of tracking. Customers will want to know the state of shipping and when to expect a package. Many options are available, including connecting the shopping cart to the shipper's tracking database, but remember this is simply a matter of informing the customer. Therefore, it will be sufficient for the shopping cart to allow loading a tracking code or tracking URL to the order details consulted by the customer. It is also desirable for the system to communicate news to customers by e-mail, for example "Your order has been shipped".

Customers will feel satisfied and comforted that the store they just purchased from is willing to take charge all the way, so make sure you inform them of exact shipping dates and provide tracking codes wherever possible –some shipping services don't support tracking.

There is still one issue to consider: while most small stores keep all their stock in one location, as the business grows you might keep several warehouses. This means goods will be shipped from different locations, maybe even from your supplier's address in some cases.

In this case, you will need the shopping cart to support loading each warehouse's address and assigning each product to a warehouse, so that these variables are considered when quoting shipping. Shopping carts seldom offer this option by default, but if your business requires it you should find out about the possibility of customizing basic functionality to accommodate a multi-warehouse schema.

Chapter 7

Digital Goods Distribution

I have mentioned digital goods distribution briefly when dealing with shopping carts for stores offering digital products. Now, let's discuss distribution procedures in more detail.

Delivery of goods is closely related to payment, more specifically to online payment authorization. Purchasers of digital goods typically expect immediate download or delivery of the product. This requires a payment system that somehow notifies your shopping cart securely that payment has been authorized. Some gateways do authorize payments online but lack a secure notification system.

Let's take the hypothetical example of gateway MyExampleGateway. It supports integration through the following web form:

```
<FORM ACTION=SOMEURL METHOD=POST>
 <INPUT   TYPE=HIDDEN   NAME=MERCHANT
VALUE=1234>
 <INPUT   TYPE=HIDDEN   NAME=IDORDER
VALUE=2001>
 <INPUT   TYPE=HIDDEN   NAME=AMOUNT
VALUE=19.90>
 <INPUT TYPE=HIDDEN NAME=APPROVEDURL
VALUE=OK.ASP>
```

```
<INPUT TYPE=SUBMIT>
</FORM>
```

When a valid payment is placed, the gateway redirects the user to the script ok.asp with the order number, transaction code, and other data. But, without the necessary security measures in place, it is not possible to add a download procedure to this signal. Why? Any site visitor can inspect the contents of the payment form, place an unpaid order, and manually execute the URL ok.asp to obtain the digital goods in the order without ever paying for them.

Therefore, automatic digital good distribution should only be enabled if the payment gateway supports secure payment approval signals.

There are several types of secure approval methods; some gateways use Silent Response. This is a secure signal from the gateway server to the shopping cart. The URL where the signal is sent is only known to the store owner, and it is never displayed during the purchase process, so there is no way for malicious visitors to find and access the script. Other combined security measures include a password to enable the Silent Response script, only known to the gateway, and several two-way communications between the cart and the gateway, for example in the case of PayPal.

Other secure methods don't include secure signals. One of them is the creation of an encrypted string based on a password stored at the gateway and the cart configuration and on other data such as order number and order amount. The gateway signal is then verified by comparing it to the encrypted string.

Lastly, a method that is becoming quite popular is sending an XML string from the shopping cart and parsing the response by means of HTTP signals hidden from the customer.

With this in mind, contact your shopping cart and gateway providers about the security measures they have available and the support they offer for digital goods distribution.

Now, let's turn to the most common types of digital good:

1) Variable digital goods
2) Fixed digital goods

The first group includes digital goods that change with each sale; for example, serial codes, calling card codes, and passwords to access restricted sections of a website. A new serial, key or password is created upon each sale.

The second group includes digital goods that remain unchanged after each sale; for example, mp3 songs , e-books, and digital photos.

The complexity of the first case is clear. Digital goods should either be created in real time, or stored and then distributed one by one, keeping records of used-up strings. In the second case, the problem is that if the digital good is heavy – mp3 files usually weigh around 4mb – you don't want to send it by e-mail, but you can't send a static link either, to avoid redistribution. The real location of the file should be hidden, and access to the file should be time-limited.

Most popular shopping carts support both scenarios, but you should confirm this functionality is available and make any necessary modifications to protect your digital goods.

A different type of digital good requires interconnection with external systems, for example when you offer support packages where you need to enable a profile in a support system. However, this case can be included in the first group: you can pre-load profiles and distribute pairs of user IDs and passwords. Then you save yourself the trouble of developing an interface between the shopping cart and the external system. Of course, this is not possible if it is absolutely necessary for the shopping cart to send signals to perform actions in external systems.

Some payment gateways support distributing digital goods right from their control panel, but this is not the best option: the functionality is quite basic, you will be tied to that provider not only for payments but also for distribution, and you will find that store management is more efficient when you deal only with one control panel, the shopping cart's.

Chapter

8

Performance And Scaling

You may be setting up an e-commerce from scratch so you have no idea how much traffic to expect, or perhaps you already have a popular site and you can make an estimation. In any case, the best advice is to prepare your store for growth. Make sure there are no immediate limitations that could turn satisfaction for the popularity gained into frustration that your e-commerce system cannot accommodate your newfound success.

An e-commerce includes many bottlenecks. Let's discuss each one in turn:

Database

Many shopping carts include an Access database to keep installation simple and allow users to test functionality quickly, without the need to embark on complicated management and configuration for a professional database. However, Access databases are limited in many ways. To start with, they can support only a certain number of concurring queries. This means that your store will function normally while visitors are few, and as concurring visits hike – precisely when you need a robust store the most- performance will decline and ultimately collapse.

Did you know that...? An Access database connected to an online store can support up to 300 concurring visits.

Also consider that some database operations take four or five times longer with Access than with a professional database. Imagine a customer performing an advanced search on your site. This operation involving several tables can take five seconds, while the same action with a professional database would take only one second to complete. The difference is significant enough that the potential customer might leave the store, under the impression that it suffers technical problems.

So, even if traffic to your store is very low, I suggest you use a professional database from day one. You will gain in performance, scalability and security.

Using a professional database also means that you can create indexes on certain fields of the most heavily-used tables, in order to increase the speed of queries and perform tuning operations for better performance.

Default shopping cart databases are usually quite generic, in the sense that they include only the bare minimum indexes and relations. You may then need additional operations to adapt the database for specific uses. For example, if you have added an Author field for your online music store, you will probably need to specify indexes to speed up searches on this field.

> Did you know that...? Databases with just a few tables and fields make it fairly obvious how to optimize queries, but more extensive databases require complex Relational Algebra. Just by moving a WHERE condition to the beginning of a query you can achieve a drastic effect on performance.

Another advantage of professional databases is that one or more servers can host them, and they can be installed out of the reach of Internet surfers. That is, the database server(s) connect to the web server through an internal network, preventing external access.

Dynamic Pages

Sites with little traffic can disregard diminished performance in dynamic pages and use all ASP or PHP pages throughout the site, even if they perform complex internal operations. However, if traffic starts picking up, you will probably need all queries optimized with fine-tuning procedures in the database and some kind of load balancing between several servers. Such solutions can be very costly, but there is a reliable alternative in using static pages or limiting the number of dynamic operations in access points.

For example:

Suppose your store can only be accessed from www.myteststore123.com and traffic is then distributed to the following pages:

Home Page: 100%
Search Page: 10%
Categories Page: 20%
Best Sellers Page: 20%
Item details: 30%
Customer login: 10%
Privacy Policy: 10%

Some operations that are complex in terms of data access can be placed on inner pages; for example, you can place a dynamic recommendations list within customer login, where only 10% of the store's original traffic will be executed. Of course these variables are neither exact nor fully quantifiable, but remember that many visitors leave the store after browsing just a few pages. The critical entry point is the access page of your domain, and this is where data access should be minimized; you can even place a static page or includes of code fragments that result from data access planned daily.

Image And Graphic Optimization

An attractive design is important, but remember that visitors to your site will be using different connection speeds and browsers. A page packed with graphics and Java applets may pose more problems than they solve. Try to compromise between design and weight: optimize graphics, making as many as possible reusable, cut big images into smaller fragments, and make sure product images are not too heavy. Also take into account that browsers usually support a limited image resolution, so it may be the same to offer a 100mb or a 1mb file.

Compiled Code

If your shopping cart works with scripting language, it may be possible to compile code to achieve better performance. Contact your shopping cart provider about this possibility.

Load Balancing

In some cases, it is necessary to share the load of traffic between several web servers. This means you can have two web servers and balance the load of concurring users between them, so that they all enjoy reasonable response time. This option should be available not only from the web server, but also from the shopping cart itself. The same Load Balancing technology can be applied to the database by means of its own tools.

Chapter

9

Fraud Prevention

You have created a website and you have managed to increase traffic, offer competitive prices, and receive considerable sales from your shopping cart every month. Still, you are ready to give up on your online store and forget about Internet selling for good. Why is that? No doubt, you are overwhelmed by cases of fraud.

When you sell on the Internet, the credit card payments you take are only provisional. That is, there is a window during which the credit card charge may be cancelled.

But delivering goods that go unpaid is not the only problem. A potential consequence of suffering too many chargebacks is having your Internet merchant account revoked.

What can be done to minimize fraud, or even wipe it out completely?

A lot can be done, provided you have the right tools.

Shopping carts provide internal fraud prevention features, and you can use third-party services for order and payment validation and related tools offered by payment gateways.

Shopping Cart Fraud Prevention Features

Shopping carts have gathered significant information on the potential customer and on the products they wish to purchase prior to the payment stage. So why not identify and reject fraudulent orders at that point?

> Did you know that...? Most frauders have nothing personal against you; they have stolen credit card information and intend to use them for as many online purchases as possible, at any store. Many of these criminals will decide not to target your store if they sense early filters to halt their actions.

Several shopping carts allow you to set a fraud prevention mode to caution or paranoid. At caution mode, your store will save suspicious orders as usual but send a warning email to the administrator. If your store is set to paranoid mode, the order will be blocked and prevented from checking out. Some shopping carts also allow you to create a "bait product" at a ridiculous price that will lure possible frauders. Fraud buyers don't intend to pay for what they purchase, so they won't mind the high price.

Other applications support the creation of a database of suspicious text strings that are typical of fraudulent orders. Especially in digital good stores, frauders tend to post orders at unusual hours when monitoring is scarce, with dummy names such as Test or John Doe, that will be blocked automatically by the shopping cart if you have configured these keywords.

Third-Party Validation Services

Internal shopping cart features are useful in helping reduce levels of fraud, but third-party service providers offer tools that can be combined to wipe out the problem completely.

One of these service providers is Precharge.

The shopping cart should send a request to the Precharge server in real time with the customer's personal information and credit card data. Precharge will return an accept or decline response based on their scoring system for transaction risk levels. Declined orders will be blocked from offline payment.

The Precharge service can also be used to validate offline credit card payments. In this case you can save time in manual processing, since fraud verification has already taken place.

Another similar service is MaxMind.

The shopping cart should send MaxMind the customer's personal information, IP address, e-mail address domain, and other useful information to assess the transaction. The MaxMind servers send a response for accept or decline in real time, after checking the information with a GeoIP geolocation metrics system, and detectors for free e-mails, frauder e-mails, anonymous proxies, and IPs from high-risk countries.

MaxMind even offers a free service to test their solution and use some filters without any monthly fees. If the number of monthly transactions reaches a certain level, you will need to migrate to a paid service plan.

Then there is a new system called TeleSign.

TeleSign is a phone verification system. Simply put, the system makes an automated call to the customer to check that the phone number entered during checkout is valid and correct. Upon answering the phone, the customer is asked to key in a code to confirm the legitimacy of the transaction.

Assuming that the customer is by the phone with the number reported, and that the phone coincides with the credit card statement address, fraud is very unlikely.

Many merchants currently selling online have used a manual equivalent of this system for a long time. That is, they have one or more employees calling customers to check that they have indeed placed an order.

Such a system of manual verification can be impractical in high-volume stores, or it is simply more economical to absorb a few cases of fraud than to hire employees for phone calls. That's why the service provided by TeleSign is so attractive.

TeleSign can be integrated with a shopping cart both at customer registration and at checkout, and it poses an interesting alternative to traditional fraud prevention methods. At the same time, it is possible and maybe even necessary to implement it in combination with other systems.

The verification phone call is originated in TeleSign's servers, and no proprietary components are required.

Gateway Fraud Prevention Tools

Payment gateways are interested in reducing fraud rates as well, so several of them support advanced fraud prevention systems. Most systems include configuring the merchant account from a proprietary control panel to decline payments that don't meet certain criteria:

- AVS: Payments can be rejected after checking the address entered by the customer against the address where the statement is delivered for the credit card number provided.
- IP: Gateways keep databases of IP addresses used for past frauds. Payments from countries with high fraud rates are usually blocked.
- CVV2: This code, printed on the back of credit cards, or sometimes on the front (for example in the case of American Express), allows you to verify that the rightful owner of the card has posted an order.

Payment gateways that don't require a merchant account, such as 2Checkout, also perform manual checks by specialized staff who may even call the potential buyer if they suspect fraud.

While the gateway is responsible for managing these systems, shopping carts should send all customer and credit card information to enable full enjoyment of fraud prevention tools. This is because gateways require some minimum data, but other information that is non-required can result in more efficient fraud screening.

Fraud should not deter you from running your online store. Choosing the right shopping cart and third-party tools will no doubt minimize occurrences of fraud to the extent that they become no more than a minor and rare concern.

Alternatives to Minimize Fraud

Online commerce does not have to be synonymous with credit card payments. In fact, many successful online stores don't take credit cards at all; credit card transactions are only a small percentage of total sales in the case of others.

Cases of fraud go unnoticed in busy stores, since they are very hard to detect among hundreds of legitimate orders. That is, criminals don't resort to sophisticated fraud techniques: they simply take advantage of the fact that not all orders can be properly monitored. An interesting way of decreasing the volume of credit card payments to be better able to monitor them is to offer alternative payment methods, which can even be made attractive to customers if necessary.

A car part store, for example, was able to decrease fraud significantly by offering a 5% off wire transfer payments. They started receiving more payments by wire transfer, requiring no verification, and employees could focus more on inspecting credit card payments closely. This simple measure practically eradicated fraud.

Even if your business can not accommodate this

schema, don't be afraid to try alternatives and offer several payment options to your customers.

In general, if you sell tangible goods and therefore delivery is delayed by shipping, you will be able to implement payment methods such as e-checks, wire transfers, and mail-in methods, which are risk-free or pose a negligible level of risk. But, if you sell digital goods, customers will want to access goods immediately after payment, so you won't be able to offer alternative payment methods. If you do, they will not be popular.

Fraud by Legitimate Customers: Chargeback Abuse

Your store has implemented all available fraud-prevention tools. All orders are monitored by automatic systems at the shopping cart, at the gateway, and by third-party systems. You also have employees calling customers personally to check orders. It all adds up; all information is correct and legitimate. However, two months later, you are notified by the gateway that a customer has placed a chargeback on an order because he claims he did not place it.

How could this happen? Many frequent Internet shoppers know that when there is no signature involved or no delivery of tangible goods to their address, they can always deny ever making a purchase. While they don't do this for every order placed, they can refuse a charge if they feel they are not receiving satisfactory service from the company or they are not happy with the quality of a product. Such action is extremely damaging to the company and it is, of course, a form of fraud.

What can be done to prevent this? First and foremost, you should have a reasonable refund policy. So, if a customer is not happy with a product or service, they can resort to the company itself and get a refund, although not necessarily for the full amount of the order.

Why would a customer rather request a partial refund than place a chargeback for the full amount? First, because they are saving the possibility of a chargeback for a case where requesting a refund is not possible. Second, because it is the right thing to do based on the terms agreed to, while he alternative is plain fraud. If not committing fraud means a 10% off a $25 payment, that is $2.50, they will probably request a refund.

If you sell tangible goods, you can request a signature acknowledging receipt of the product purchased, securing documented proof to dispute a chargeback. If you sell digital goods or services, you can request a signed document, for example a contract or list of conditions, to be sent with each order.

Another idea is to implement a Chargeback Abuse policy. If laws in your country or state allow it, you can reserve the right to share information on orders with chargeback, so that the frauder is added to a black list database, making it difficult for them to make other online purchases in the future.

While the above measures can help minimize

occurrences of fraudulent chargebacks, remember that it is always the purchaser that has the power, and any store taking credit card payments online is bound to face this problem sooner or later.

Under the current policies for online payments, sellers bear all the burden of fraudulent purchases. Not only do they suffer having delivered products and services that are never paid for, but they are also liable for penalties imposed by the payment gateway, they incur the shipping charges, and they risk losing their merchant accounts. Credit card companies should update their policies to create a system that is fairer and more predictable for all parties involved. A good system for one-time (non-recurring) payments would be to standardize merchants' policies, eliminate the possibility of placing a chargeback, and require some form of reliable authentication at the time of payment. For example, store A accepts refunds only within 10 days after a sale. When a customer places an order, they know they will not be able to request a refund after that period. Since chargebacks can not be placed, the customer's only choice to refuse the charge will be to report the card as stolen and claim that authentication was cracked. Then they would be forced to go through paperwork, or they would have to pay a card replacement fee. Such a schema would prevent most instances of chargeback abuse.

Chapter 10

Increasing Sales

You have your store all set up, sales are coming in, it is secure and robust, but you find from sales reports that billing has hit a slump in the last few months.

Is it possible to sell more? Of course, and you may already have the tools to accomplish it, even if you have never regarded them as sales-related.

So, get your creative juices going and reflect on your own experience as an online shopper.

Traffic

It is valid to view sales as a percentage of visits to your store. This percentage is known as Closure Rate: the rate of shoppers that actually turn into Buyers. The obvious conclusion is that increased traffic will result in increased sales.

> Note: Of course, this premise is true only of traffic that is relevant to your store. If you sell screws, traffic referred from a search engine where the keyword was "children's books" will do very little for your sales.

There is more than one way to increase traffic; you con reorganize your site to be better ranked in search engines, purchase keywords from Google and other portals, build an affiliate network, and distribute newsletters. All are valid and useful ways of attracting more visitors to your store.

Ranking in Search Engines

Efficient use of search engine rankings is not as simple as it may seem. It is usual for companies to enjoy great rankings for static pages with corporate information, and at the same time suffer low rankings, or none at all, in searches for the specific products or services they offer.

This happens because search engines use complex algorithms to assess the relevance of sites and of each section within a site. Corporate information pages usually do well because they are static, contain a lot of text that can be located by indexing applications, and include tags with descriptions and keywords that are hidden from the visitor.

On the other hand, the dynamic catalog pages created by shopping carts will seldom achieve good results unless the following variables been taken into account:

> 1) Meta Tags: Web pages contain information records (Meta Tags) invisible to visitors but used by search engines to categorize the website. Your shopping cart should include these Meta Tags in such a way that your site can be indexed

thoroughly: not only your shopping cart's front page, but the whole catalog, should be indexed.

2) Keywords: Within Meta Tags you can mention keywords which will determine under which searches the page will come up. The shopping cart should allow you to define keywords for the store's general pages, but also specific keywords for each product's details page. For example: if you load an Umax 1220P scanner you can include the keywords: scanner, scanning, umax, u-max, etc.

3) Static page generating: many search engines don't index dynamic pages with .asp or .jsp extension, for example, or rank them poorly compared to static pages. So it's possible that none of your catalog's pages will be indexed. The problem is solved by generating an HTML index for all products in the catalog as well as an HTML page for each product. The static pages generated include all meta tags and keywords as well as links to the shopping cart's dynamic processes. Therefore a customer may reach the store through one of these static pages and then proceed to the shopping cart's dynamic actions: search, category listing, auctions, etc.

4) Affiliate links: since the introduction of Google, many search engines judge the relevance of a site from the amount of other sites with links pointing to the original site. But, how can you get other sites to display links to yours without having to plead? Affiliate programs. You

should allow any store visitor to sign up as an affiliate. They will get a link, code snippets and a page with available banners. With this information affiliates can add links in their sites and create a winning situation for both parties: you get more traffic, a better ranking in search engines, and more sales, while the affiliate gets a commission for each sale. It is also useful to allow affiliates to sign up automatically without any intervention by the store administrator: adding a certain amount of affiliates manually each week could prove impractical, plus a delay in getting the code snippets will usually discourage other site owners from joining the affiliate program.

Auction Sites

An alternative and attractive source of traffic is auction sites such as eBay. Not all products and services are suitable for auction but, if yours are, make sure you look into this possibility.

> Note: Posting your products on auction sites doesn't necessarily mean that they will be auctioned off at any price, hurting your reputation. In fact, most auctions have a fixed price defined. The customer pledges to purchase the product at a fixed price, just like they would within your e-commerce site.

Basic integration with an auction site is creating an account and loading product details manually. Potential buyers place a bid, and the winner of the auction contacts you to arrange payment, that can be set up from your store.

Some shopping carts support export of all or part of your catalog directly through the eBay API. It is amazing the amount of traffic you can obtain thanks to this functionality.

Remember, however, that there may be minimum fees for publishing and a percentage of the selling price may be due to the auction site. You will find that fees are insignificant compared to the benefits.

Price Comparison Systems

As I mentioned previously, this is another excellent tool for increasing sales. If your products are suitable for price comparison systems, you can export your catalog and get your products listed. Suppose someone is interested in purchasing a specific digital camcorder. They will first consult a service such as Pricegrabber, Shopping.com, or Froogle to find the best price available including shipping. Then they might read customer reviews, since many of the listed stores may not be well known. Therefore, if your store offers good prices and quality service, you have every chance of attracting higher sales by this means. Products that respond especially well to price comparison systems include electronics, photography devices, computers, toys, and books. Make sure your prices are updated regularly; export your files to comparison systems whenever there is a change in your catalog.

Newsletters

Just by having a list of your store's sales you have also a list of e-mail addresses where you can send messages about special offers. Design a promotion with attractive benefits, extract the addresses that may be relevant, and distribute a newsletter with discount codes or details on the promotion. It is very likely that the campaign will result in new sales and revive the interest of past customers in your products. Remember customers hate being hassled by e-mail, so don't overdo the number of campaigns and of course include opt-out capabilities.

Reward Points

Supply for some products is so extensive these days, that it is common for shoppers to switch providers on a daily basis. They don't think twice before purchasing from a different store just because a price has dropped. Therefore, it is vital that you design an efficient strategy to create loyalty.

Do your number and implement a point system where customers can pay for future orders partly with points they have earned. Many shopping carts support this option, whether with a specific feature or manual discount codes and offline point calculation.

E-mail to Friend

Casual visitors may find a product or service interesting, but be too lazy to write down the information on the site. With the simple possibility of sending item details by e-mail by clicking on the famous "E-mail To Friend" button, you will be attracting a future visit and maybe even a sale.

Recommendations

Many stores have extensive catalogues, and sometimes customers are not willing to spend time performing detailed searches and surfing through thousands of products until they find one they need. An automatic recommendations system is useful in these cases. This feature typically tracks historic orders and produces a list of recommended products based on different criteria such as category, price range, and sale items.

Customer Reviews

The relationship between user recommendations and sales can be hard to see. Some merchants are even scared of facing negative or untruthful reviews. Nevertheless, in practice, publishing reviews is a great tool for sales, for several reasons. First, user reviews are search engine-friendly content. Second, users often seek independent reviews and may end up becoming customers on your own site. Third, harmful reviews are no longer a great concern because they can be moderated prior to publishing.

Don't hesitate: place a customer reviews system, moderate messages if you are wary of misuse, and promote the posting of reviews among your customers.

Visit Analysis

In order to determine the efficiency of the measures you implement, you must use a statistics system on your store. While hosting services do offer this type of system, the information they produce is usually irrelevant to the analysis of traffic on the e-commerce channel.

The information you need includes:

1) Total and unique visits, excluding company staff visits
2) Visits to individual products
3) Search strings in the shopping cart search function
4) Origin of store visitors

If necessary, install and set up an e-commerce-specific statistics system, and only track stats for the information that will be useful to your assessment.

Chapter

11

Security

A small business in the publishing industry decides to start selling retail on the web. The webmaster contacts the hosting service provider and is delighted to learn that the service includes a PHP shopping cart free of charge. He installs the shopping cart from the hosting control panel and within minutes he starts loading the catalog books and setting his preferences.

While the managers sign up for a Merchant Account and decide on a payment gateway, the webmaster configures an off-line credit card system in order to start selling right away.

They launch an ad campaign with banners and the Google AdWords system, and the store starts getting visits. The implementation turns out to be a huge success: sales amount to $1,150 the first month, much more than expected.

The following month the trouble starts: some customers call with complaints that after purchasing the books their credit cards received many additional charges; other people claim that they have been charged for books they haven't bought and that have been shipped to PO Boxes. At the same time notices related to fraudulent sales start pouring in: threats to ban them from getting card payments and letters from lawyers threatening to sue for fraud, privacy violation and lack of data protection. Just when they think nothing else can possibly go wrong, the whole catalog is suddenly deleted and the shopping cart home page is replaced with offensive messages stating that the store has been hacked.

The webmaster then uninstalls the shopping cart and hires a computer security consultant to diagnose the situation. The specialist's report states that the attackers have taken advantage of several vulnerabilities of the shopping cart.

First they launched a dictionary attack on the control panel login, gaining access to a list with customers' information. Since credit card numbers remained in the database after transactions, the attackers got hold of this data as well.

Later, other attackers did an SQL Injection deleting all products and inserting a product with offensive messages in the home page.

The shopping cart also had other flaws which allowed customers to change the prices of purchased products without the webmaster ever noticing the change.

The main mistake in this case was the lack of precaution when implementing the online store. While it is true that the installed PHP shopping cart had security flaws and lacked measures to prevent attacks, the main responsibility rested on the webmaster.

He could have avoided most problems by taking very simple measures such as:

1) Searching the web for vulnerabilities of the shopping cart in general and his version in particular
2) Contacting the cart developers for installation and customization advice related to increasing security, as well as patches for known vulnerabilities
3) Deciding, based on his findings, whether that shopping cart was the best choice to sell online
4) Consulting a computer security specialist as far as the budget allowed

An e-commerce application is a tool designed to sell and increase profitability. Security issues deriving from flaws in the software itself go against this ultimate goal. Therefore it is very important for e-commerce component developers to consider security measures and provide tips on how to avoid most common problems.

Check for the following features in e-commerce software:

1) Dictionary attack prevention with profile blocking for the control panel
2) Prevention from SQL Injection attacks in high-risk sensitive areas
3) Password and sensitive information encryption with RC4 and DES algorithms
4) Support for credit card record deletion after transactions are processed
5) Detailed recording of catalog stock operations
6) Snapshot of each sale to verify the amount charged for each product in each order
7) Support for blocking purchases from free e-

mail addresses and orders with suspicious text strings

8) Support for blocking customers who have performed chargebacks and/or troublesome customers

9) Recording and viewing the last login at the control panel

10) Recording customers' IP with each order

11) Global customer password resetting when threatened by intrusion

12) Support for closing the store with one click and avoiding checkouts in order to diagnose trouble

13) Delivery of database error reports to the administrator by e-mail or SMS

We can then ask ourselves whether choosing a shopping cart with a series of security measures is enough to guarantee a secure implementation. The answer is plainly: no.

Security requires constant action and is not limited to taking measures during implementation. Imagine a vulnerability is discovered in your Web Server or your database. The attacker could access sensitive information without ever touching your shopping cart. If a flaw is exploited in the payment gateway you use, your business would be exposed and this would not be related to the shopping cart. Even if a user chooses the most secure shopping cart, if they don't read the documentation and security advice, and if they keep default settings, they will be putting their e-commerce implementation at risk.

Choosing a security-minded shopping cart is important but not enough. Store administrators should follow security advice during installation, stay permanently in touch with software developers, and subscribe to lists with vulnerability reports. They should constantly monitor the use of the cart and perform regular controls in search of warning signs.

In conclusion, the right choice of shopping cart combined with a proactive and informed attitude is the key to years of uneventful online sales and excellent profitability.

Chapter 12

Technical Support

E-commerce systems are usually made up of several components: the shopping cart, the payment gateway, the hosting service, the shipping quoting provider, and the database, among others.

If a problem comes up, it is important that you have support information readily available. Imagine your store that sells men's apparel is enjoying great sales a week before Father's Day and, just when you need it the most, your e-commerce system simply stops working. You will have to dig into your e-mails to find support details for each component, and once you are in contact you will probably be requested your order number or customer code. In some cases you will use a web support system, in others e-mail, in others the phone... Finding all this information at once could be very time-consuming, not to mention you will be losing more money the longer your e-commerce awaits support. It is also possible that the store administrator is unable to access the e-mail from which the services were hired. In a nutshell, getting out of an emergency can be more complicated than it seems.

The smartest thing to do, then, is to plan for a contingency. First make a tidy list, in order of importance, with an entry for each component, including support policy, contact method, user identification, order number, and the scope of each component.

For example:

1.

```
Component: shopping cart
Support policy: Monday to Friday, 9
am to 6 pm, remote diagnosis by
technicians included
Contact method: web support form
User identification: customer code
XBAAA123
Scope of the component: provided
access to the site is available, any
error related to catalog browsing
and checkout procedure until payment
screen
```

2.

```
Component: hosting service
Support policy: 24x7, support
limited to recommendations and
instructions
Contact method: phone
User identification: domain
MyStore.com
Scope of the component: website
access, e-mail accounts, database
```

Follow the same procedure for each component. In the event of an emergency, it will be extremely useful to have all this information combined in one place.

Other matters come into play, of course. In my experience at the head of software companies I have seen that users in desperate need of help do very little to help themselves. A phone call saying "my e-commerce system is not working" is not very useful and can only be the starting point to diagnose a problem. After many comings and goings the technician might be able to diagnose the source of the problem and solve it. In the case of e-mail or web support the first communication is even more critical, since each question and answer can take several hours. So, what should do the store administrator do before requesting support?

The store administrator should gather all the information available on the incident. Useful information for diagnosis includes:

- A description of the problem in plain language
- Errors displayed by internal diagnosing systems, if any
- Does the problem come up always under the same circumstances? Is it random? Or is it impossible to determine the causes of the problem?
- Have you made any modifications recently that might be related?
- If it applies: What version is your software? Which payment gateway have you configured?
- If it applies: What is your system configuration? (environment, database, optional packages)

With this information handy, the technician will probably be able to diagnose the problem instantly and save you lots of time –and money.

Many customers base their decisions to hire services and companies exclusively on the availability of pone support. This option sometimes means customers call before taking the time to gather the necessary information for support staff. Other risks are that explanations or recommendations can be misunderstood, and there are no records of solutions provided. Therefore, although it may not seem that way, it may be better to go for a web support system with good response time and a form that prompts you to enter the data necessary to diagnose a problem.

Regarding support requests, it is better to limit the number of component providers for your e-commerce system. If your shopping cart provider also hosts your site and your database, you will have fewer contacts to juggle and you won't face a situation where no one is willing to take responsibility for a problem.

Finally, consider that many technical issues can be diagnosed and solved in-house. Without going so far as to hiring a specialized programmer, you can train your webmaster or yourself, if you are running the site, by taking a course that provides you with the tools to act in a case of emergency with corrective actions or temporary patches. Knowledge will be your most precious asset to understand the source of problems and make economical and sound decisions.

Innovation

The Internet is packed with millions of online stores. Customers are no longer loyal to the companies they do business with, and they will easily switch providers if they can better process, if they feel more comfortable, or even if their online shopping experience is more pleasant.

Of course, any e-commerce system must fulfill a series of standard functions such as supporting online payments, providing accurate shipping quotes, and offering a shopping experience that is as simple and user-friendly as possible. But, there are many other features that may seem over-the-top, which may well be the key to running a successful store.

This is the case of Amazon's Gold Box^{TM}, a small treasure chest with offers valid during a short period of time, and One Step Checkout, allowing a customer to finalize a purchase in only one sep. Neither feature seems vital at first glance; however, they have succeeded in grabbing customers' attention and keeping them loyal.

You will surely find additional features that can be applied to your industry as added value for the shopping experience.

During a training course for the administrator of an auto parts store, we presented a new development for a WAP store; i.e. a parallel store that presented the e-commerce catalog to any customer with a cell phone with WAP browser. The administrator explained that many of his customers were mechanics who quoted repairs at their clients' premises, so it was very useful for them to check prices, and even to place orders for the spare parts, from right there. With some modifications to the default WAP store, he was able to increase sales significantly by offering a benefit above and beyond what other online auto parts store could offer: it was not a matter of price, but of better service.

I also remember the case of a company that sold toner refills for laser printers. They had reached a bottleneck where they could not ship orders any faster. The reason turned out to be that staff consulted the store's control panel with a complicated login system, they left the computer for a few hours to prepare the package, and when they came back the application had timed out, so they had to start over. The system was replaced with flashing signs that displayed order details and a barcode reader that was used to load shipping information for the order. This did the trick to speed up delivery of goods to customers.

Innovation, as you can see above, can be related either to the storefront or backoffice, that is the system used within the company. Also take into account that any e-commerce product or service you purchase or hire must allow modifications with as little fuss as possible.

Canned applications include most common functions and they can be adapted to any industry but, sooner or later, a higher degree of innovation will be needed.

Innovation can consist of integrating several systems and bringing in electronic equipment, such as flashing signs, or no more than small internal developments. An example of this last case is a used watch retailer that achieved a sales boost just by offering an enhanced viewing system for the used luxury watches that included rotation and zoom. The modification took under one day to develop, but its effect on sales was astonishing.

In conclusion, even if your store is considerable successful, don't be afraid to innovate: use your imagination, request input from your customers, explore other e-commerce sites, ask your product and service providers what can be achieved with the latest enhancements. The results can be beyond satisfactory.

Chapter

14

Conclusions and Acknowledgments

We have now reached the end of the book: some topics were probably left out, but I hope you have found here a practical guide to achieving success in e-commerce. I am also creating a point of contact to receive any experiences you would like to share about following the advice in the book. Feel free to send any comments and suggestions to book@comersus.com, where all messages will be read and considered.

I would like to thank Darío Paniagua for his valuable input to the chapter on Site Design, Contents and Structure.

Another big thank you goes out to all Comersus shopping cart users and customers. Some of you may not know that Comersus shopping cart is actually the result of a failure. In the early 90's I decided to leave my job in IT and set up my own business with some partners, attracted by the promise of e-commerce growth in South America. With the bursting of the dotcom bubble, our company went down as did many others in South America and the world. Despite the company going bankrupt, the product I had developed was robust and far better than other e-commerce solutions widely available at the time. So, I decided to turn a failure into something positive and I launched the shopping cart publicly under the name Comersus Cart.

At first, the whole venture amounted to just a web site, a beeper under my pillow, and a passion for development and innovation. The beeper would ring at 3 AM and I would jump out of bed to sit at the computer and provide support to users. With time, that passion attracted to Comersus the work of other developers in the world who had benefited from the use of the free e-commerce software and wished to contribute to the project in appreciation. Then came a business restructuring where I started offering paid enhancement packages and hired professionals to provide permanent sales assistance and quality technical support. Soon after, I was contacted by companies in the US and elsewhere that were interested in distributing Comersus solutions to reach more specific markets. Within the schema of distribution agreements we started offering training courses to explain the capabilities of the software. It was in relation to these courses that I started writing down some documents with information that was valuable but yet untapped. Comersus distributors and other advanced users that I am in constant contact with encouraged me to put together the experiences lived together, first in individual documents, and now in the form of a book.

My appreciation, then, goes out to all Comersus Cart users and customers and to the staff that works with me at Comersus Open Technologies. All of them and their faith in me helped me offer my "insider" advice to achieve success in e-commerce.

Rodrigo Alhadeff
September, 2005

Chapter 15

Glossary

HTML: Hypertext Markup Language. The document-formatting language used in the WWW.

CVV2: A 3 to 4 digit security code used in credit cards to minimize fraud.

SSL: Secure Sockets Layer. A protocol developed by Netscape to transmit private data over the Internet.

AVS: Address Verification System. A system that compares the address entered by a customer to the credit card statement address.

HTTPS: A protocol that supports secure communications over the Internet.

mySQL: An Open Source database.

SQL Server: A Microsoft database.

Web Server: A software application that allows users to access the contents of static web pages, or pages generated by the execution of dynamic scripts.

FTP: File Transfer Protocol. A protocol designed to transfer files between machines.

ASP: Active Server Pages. A scripting language developed by Microsoft that supports creating dynamic websites with data access.

PHP: A scripting language that supports creating dynamic websites.

Merchant Account: A bank account that is opened in order to take credit card payments.

Meta-Tags: Information that is hidden from the view of browsers, located in the header of an HTML page.

IP: A number identifying a computer or device on the Internet.

SMS: Short Message Service. Text messages up to 160 characters long, available on GSM telephone networks and others.

SQL: A language used to execute operations on databases.

www.ingramcontent.com/pod-product-compliance
Lightning Source LLC
Chambersburg PA
CBHW051255050326
40689CB00007B/1199